FROM THE AUTHOR OF 31 DAYS TO A GREATER UNDERSTANDING OF MONEY

MONEY
MATTERS

MOTIVATION, METHODS, AND MANNERS FOR INCREASE!

MASTER FINANCIAL COACH
KAREN FORD

Copyright © 2018 Karen Ford

MONEY MATTERS

Printed in the USA

Published by KBF Management Company, Fairmont, WV

Prepared for publication by www.wendykwalters.com

ISBN (print): 978-0-9995415-2-4

ISBN (kindle): 978-0-9995415-3-1

Library of Congress Control Number (LCCN): 2018943005

All Rights Reserved. This book is protected by the copyright laws of the United States of America. This book may not be copied or reprinted for commercial gain or profit. The use of short quotations is permitted. Permission will be granted upon request. The author guarantees all contents are original and do not infringe upon the legal rights of any other person or work.

Portions of scripture taken from the *English Standard Version* are marked ESV. Copyright © 2001 by Crossway Bibles, a division of Good News Publishers. Used by permission. All rights reserved.

Portions of scripture taken from the King James Version are marked KJV. Originally published in 1611, this Bible is in the public domain.

Portions of scripture taken from the *The Message* are marked MSG. by Eugene H. Peterson. Copyright © 1993, 1994, 1995, 1996, 2000, 2001, 2002. Used by permission of NavPress Publishing Group.

Portions of scripture taken from the *New American Standard Bible* are marked NASB. Copyright © 1960, 1962, 1963, 1968, 1971, 1972, 1973, 1975, 1977, 1995 by The Lockman Foundation. Used by permission.

Portions of scripture taken from the *New English Translation (The NET Bible)* are designated NET. Scripture quoted by permission. Copyright © 1996-2006 by Biblical Studies Press. All rights reserved.

Portions of scripture taken from the *Holy Bible, New International Version*, NIV® are marked NIV. Copyright © 1973, 1978, 1984 by the International Bible Society. Used by permission of Zondervan Publishing House. All rights reserved. The "NIV" and "New International Version" are trademarks registered

Portions of scripture taken from the New King James Version are marked NKJV. Copyright © 1979, 1980, 1982 by Thomas Nelson, Inc. Used by permission. All rights reserved.

Portions of scripture taken from The Holy Bible, New Living Translation are marked NLT. Copyright © 1996. Used by permission by Tyndale House Publishers, Inc., Wheaton, IL. All rights reserved.

DEDICATION

This book is dedicated to a variety of people, of which I am so very thankful. Mere words on paper can't express my gratitude for you all.

- JOE FORD: To my husband who has been so very patient with me throughout this writing process and continues to believe in me—priceless! Thank you for your love for me.

- PAUL AND NORMA WHITE: To my parents who not only believe in me but have raised me to be good with money. Their example through the years has spoken louder to me than words!

- DR. JOHN AND DR. REBECCA POLIS: To my spiritual parents who have believed in me for over 26 years. I am able to do what I'm doing because of you. I am so grateful for you both!

WHAT OTHERS ARE SAYING

Based on scriptural principles, *Money Matters* provides sound teaching and practical guidance for learning how to manage finances, overcome debt, and invest in the future. Karen gives hope and positive direction to those looking for solutions to financial woes to be able to live the favored life God desires for His children.

—NORMA WHITE
RETIRED TEACHER

This is written with so much practical application while increasing your faith. Everyone would benefit from this book.

—DEBBIE CROSTON
ASCENSION MINISTRIES

I have discovered that there are several different paths and plans needed to build wealth and to get out of bad-debt. Karen Ford has written a great book sharing one of those plans that is designed more for the average person to move out of financial bondage and into financial freedom. Great job!

—DR. KEITH JOHNSON
AMERICA'S #1 CONFIDENCE COACH

Inside these pages you will find sensible, down-to-earth advice for paying down debt and building passive income. The information is approachable and pragmatic, written openly and with an eye toward building your faith and expanding your ability to walk in generosity.

—WENDY K. WALTERS
FAVOR FOUNDATION

> "Every time you borrow money, you're robbing your future self."
>
> —NATHAN W. MORRIS

CONTENTS

Foreword by Dr. John Polis   ix
Foreword by Dr. Rebecca Polis   xi

INTRODUCTION   1

Chapter 1 - Does God Want Me to Be Prosperous?   3
Chapter 2 - The 10% Factor   15
Chapter 3 - How Did We Get Into Debt?   27
Chapter 4 - Help, I'm Overwhelmed!   37
Chapter 5 - Debt Demolition   49
Chapter 6 - Don't Be Passive About Your Income   59
Chapter 7 - Kids and Money   67

FINAL WORDS   73

> "The strength of your personal financial resources is equivalent to the quality of your financial decision making."
>
> —WAYNE CHIRISA

FOREWORD BY DR. JOHN POLIS

Karen Ford's newest book, *Money Matters*, has hit the mark on telling the Bible's truth about money. I like the title because **money really does matter** in terms of how we relate to God and live out this life on earth in a way that glorifies Him. Jesus taught us that God has only one serious competition when it comes to our affections when He made the statement, "You can not love God and mammon, you will hate the one and love the other" (Luke 16:11-13).

How we handle money is a direct reflection of our revelation of God's ownership and our stewardship. It is the tool God uses test our value system and loyalty to Him. It reveals our capacity to steward resources and revelation. After leading churches and ministries for 38 years at this time, I have never seen a Christian come fully into God's best for their life who didn't understand and follow correct biblical teaching on money.

The journey of the Children of Israel from Egypt to the Promised Land gives us a good illustration to learn from regarding God's plan for abundant financial blessings. Egypt was the "land of not enough." The wilderness was a "land of just enough," but Canaan was the "land of more than enough." God's will is for us all to live in the "more than enough" Land of Promise where we will be blessed and a become a blessing to others. Read and practice what Karen has given us in *Money Matters* and you will arrive in your financial Canaan in time.

—JOHN POLIS
FOUNDER AND PRESIDENT, REVIVAL FELLOWSHIP INTERNATIONAL
JOHN POLIS MINISTRIES, FAITH CHURCH NETWORK

> "There are several things to be learned about money from Scripture, and the concepts of generosity and giving are in there."
>
> —DAVE RAMSEY

FOREWORD BY DR. REBECCA POLIS

This book is a WEALTH of financial knowledge. It is personal, practical, positive, and very powerful. The Scriptures say that the truth will set you free and most assuredly the truths contained herein will enjoyably educate you, motivate you, and empower you to live at a desirable level of financial security and independence.

I appreciate Karen's search for God's true meaning of words—they are enlightening! Karen's practical approach to the things of God make them accessible to every believer. No matter where you are in your faith walk or your financial journey, this book will be an encouragement to you.

Thank you Karen Ford for writing a book that will enable those who read it to come to new levels of financial freedom!

—REBECCA POLIS
COACH, TEACHER
CO-FOUNDER OF FAITH CHURCH INTERNATIONAL

> "Owe no one anything except to love one another, for he who loves another has fulfilled the law."
>
> —ROMANS 13:8, NKJV

Introduction

Many people are in the place where they want to get out of debt and desire to build wealth, but sadly they don't know where to begin. Their hearts are in the right place. Certainly, a desire to get out of debt and to build wealth is quite valid.

Some, not only don't know where to begin, but wonder if they can. They wonder if God wants them to be wealthy. They wonder if "they" are the ones that are going to be stuck in poverty, lack, or destined to live a life less than they want.

Does God want me to have money? If so, why? How do I get the money that God wants me to have?

This book not only will answer the question if God wants you to have money, but gives practical insight and steps to demolish debt and principles in building wealth.

This book is entitled "Money Matters" because it not only discusses various matters surrounding money, but the reader will also discover that money really does matter.

CHAPTER 1

Does God Want Me To Be Prosperous?

When it comes to money, most people would say that they would like to make more money and to have more money, so they can live more comfortably and even give more to the Kingdom of God. A question that crosses their mind is this: "Does God want me to have more money?" Some folks are unsure of the answer to this question.

Jesus talked more about money than He did Heaven or hell. In fact, there are more than 2,500 Bible verses pertaining to money, yet some folks wonder if God wants **them** to prosper. The best place we can locate the answer is in the Word of God.

Most people think "money" when they hear the word "prosperity." But prosperity covers several areas in our lives. It covers our health, marriages, families, relationships but certainly includes the topic of money. The word "prosper" means 'to excel in that which is desirable.'

We note that God wants us to excel in all of these areas!

"Beloved, I wish above all things that thou mayest prosper and be in health, even as thy soul prospereth" (3 John 2 KJV). We see in this verse that God wants us to prosper in every area of our lives, and this includes the area of our finances.

I struggled with this verse for many years. I was brought up in a home, where I had loving parents and six siblings. Both of my parents worked very hard, and we had our needs met, but there wasn't always extra money for the additional toy, or new gadget that the other neighborhood children had. After I got saved, I read this verse, but my thoughts wondered if this included me. Did this verse apply to my life? Did God want me to be prosperous? And if He did, why wasn't I walking in those blessings of prosperity? Why was I living paycheck to paycheck? Did God love other people more than me and that's why they had so much more than me? Certainly, I knew that was wrong thinking, because God is love and He could not love others more. His love is unconditional and never ending, and it's the same for everyone. But why was I struggling with money, paying my bills, and always seemed to be in lack?

Since I was in lack, how was I supposed to attain more?

In Deuteronomy 8:18, we're told: "And you shall remember the Lord your God, for it is He who gives you power to get wealth, that He may establish His covenant which He swore to your fathers, as it is this day."

In this passage, God wants us to remember Him! The word "remember" in the Hebrew means, "to be mindful of, boast, consider, make mention, take thought, and confess."

God wants us to call to mind, boast, and make mention of what He has already done.

When I was a child, I recall at Christmas time receiving presents and how excited I was to open the packages, and the sheer anticipation with which I opened them. I could hardly wait to dive in to those gifts to see what was in them! Once the gift was unwrapped, I would shout with excitement about playing with the new toy, or wearing new clothing and showing my friends what my dad and mom bought me. That is what our heavenly Father wants. He wants us to shout with excitement and rejoice in what He has given us and what He has done. In fact, He wants us to be excited even before we open them!

When we **remember** the Lord, we are boasting and making mention with excitement what He has done!

The word power in this scripture is a Hebrew word, "koach" and it means "force, might, strength and ability."

God not only wants us to prosper, but He gives us the force, the might, the strength and the ability to do so. Why would God give us power to get wealth if He didn't want us to be wealthy? Selah.

We also see the word wealth is a Hebrew word, "chayil" and it means "forces, riches, strength, and means or other resources."

God has not only given us the ability to **create** wealth but He also wants us to **have** wealth. He wants us to possess it!

This is where a lot of Christians have struggled. They read this verse and note that God does want us to have wealth, but then they wonder if this verse applies to them. The answer is YES!

> "Let them shout for joy and be glad, who favor my righteous cause; and let them say continually, "Let the Lord be magnified, Who has pleasure in the prosperity of His servant."

PS 35:27 NKJV

This verse is telling us that God wants us to be prosperous! God is well pleased when we are prosperous! How pleased is He?

The word "pleasure" means "delight" or "pleased with." God is delighted and pleased with us when we prosper. He wants us to prosper, because it brings Him joy. Those that are parents, when your children walk in what they are called to be and do, it pleases and delights your heart. That is what happens with God when we walk in prosperity.

When we read Scriptures we see that money can either be a blessing or a curse. This is because if you focus on money as your main objective, and place it ahead of God, then it's going to be disastrous. What, I thought you said that God wants me to have money? He does!

In other words, God doesn't want anything to be placed above Him.

But if we put God first He will multiply our blessings, and this includes money.

We can see this in the stories of Abraham, Joseph, Job and others. They were blessed financially because of their faithfulness to God. Some of them even experienced setbacks, their wealth increased over what they already had. This was because they remained faithful and placed God ahead of money. So, God does want you to have money, but He doesn't want money to have you!

God wants you to prosper. God wants you to have money!

Let's look at a few reasons why God wants you to have money.

GOD WANTS TO BLESS YOU!

Psalm 84:11 in the Amplified Bible says:

> *"For the Lord God is a Sun and Shield; the Lord bestows [present] grace and favor and [future] glory (honor, splendor, and heavenly bliss)! No good thing will He withhold from those who walk uprightly."*

God's WORD Translation says it this way:

> *"... He does not hold back any blessing ..."*

Psalm 115:14 in the Amplified Bible says:

> *"May the Lord give you increase more and more, you and your children."*

Personally, I struggled with this concept. I knew God loved me and I knew that God wanted to bless people. My struggle was "Did God want to bless me?" It was easier for me to believe that God would bless others than believe that God wanted to bless me.

Folks, this is a lie of the enemy that he wants us to believe. The enemy comes to steal, kill and destroy. If the enemy can convince you that you're not to have money, then you won't believe that you can have it!

I had to begin believing the Truth of God's Word that He not only wanted to meet needs and bless others, but He also wanted to meet my needs and bless me!

See, if the enemy can convince you that God will bless others and not you, then you won't press in to God's Word or walk in obedience to His Word to attain His promises.

We must believe, confess, and obey God's Word so we can walk out His promises, which includes His blessings of prosperity! Don't come into agreement with the idea that you have to live in lack.

JESUS CAME TO GIVE YOU ABUNDANT LIFE, NOT ABUNDANT LACK!

> *"The thief does not come except to steal, and to kill, and to destroy. I have come that they may have life, and that they may have it more abundantly."*
>
> JOHN 10:10 NKJV

I've heard some people say that they're always in a financial lack situation and wonder why God isn't blessing them. Beloved, it says right here that it is the enemy who steals, kills and destroys. God doesn't want you to live in lack. That is the enemy, the devil! We have a real thief that we must guard against.

> God's purpose is to give us a rich, satisfying life

In the NLT, it says that God's purpose is to give us a rich, satisfying life.

God isn't sitting in Heaven with a desire that we "we just get by" in life.

You, as a parent don't want your children to just get by. How much more does your Heavenly Father want that for you? God wants you to have a great life, an abundant life! Say this with me, "God wants me to have an abundant life!" Say this over and over until you know that you know that this is truth!

HE WANTS YOU TO HAVE YOUR NEEDS MET!

Another reason why God blesses is to be sure to supply your needs.

> *"And my God will supply all your needs according to His riches in glory in Christ Jesus."*
>
> PHIL 4:19 NASB

This is comforting because it doesn't say that God might, but God *will*! This means everything! All! He will meet ***all*** of your needs! Now it's according to His riches. It doesn't say that God will meet all your needs according to your job, or according to your paycheck. NO! He will meet all of your needs according to His riches! HE has abundance of resources and an inexhaustible supply. The earth is the Lords and the fullness thereof. He is well able to get resources to you!

GOD'S DESIRE IS FOR HIS CHILDREN TO BE RICH!

> *"For ye know the grace of our Lord Jesus Christ, that, though he was rich, yet for your sakes he became poor, that ye through his poverty might be rich."*
>
> 2 CORINTHIANS 8:9

Jesus left Heaven, with all of its abundance, gold, riches, to come to earth in a flesh body. He left the rich and became poor. Now, this isn't to say that Jesus walked this earth poor and in lack. He did not live in lack while He was here on earth in a physical body. But, He did leave Heaven and came to earth- So comparably, He did become poor, because He left Heaven in all of its opulence and riches.

The evidence that Jesus was not poor or in lack when He was here as a physical man, was that He had a treasurer. A person wouldn't need a treasurer if He were poor or in lack! You don't generally have an account for a few cents.

The word "rich" is the Greek word "plousios" which means wealthy and abounding with.' Abounding with what? Abounding with material resources.

The word "rich" appears a second time in this verse and it is the Greek word "plouteo," which means, "to be rich, to have abundance, increased with goods, affluent in resources so that he can give blessings of salvation to all."

God wants you to live in abundance. He not only wants you to have all of your needs met, but He wants you to have even MORE!

Jesus said:

> *"If you then, being evil, know how to give good gifts to your children, how much more will your Father who is in heaven give good things to those who ask Him."*
>
> MATT 7:11 NKJV

As a parent, you want your children to be blessed, prosperous, not just have their needs met. You don't want them to lack. You don't want them to have just enough to get by.

Our Heavenly Father desires that not only our needs get met, but to have our desires, wants, "gifts" given to us.

He is saying that He WANTS to give us those things that we desire.

He wants you to be prosperous!

GOD WANTS YOU BLESSED FINANCIALLY TO HELP FUND THE GOSPEL.

"And you shall remember the Lord your God, for it is He who gives you power to get wealth, that He may establish His covenant which He swore to your fathers, as it is this day."

DEUT 8:18 NKJV

We need to understand this verse gives us four things God wants.

We must **remember** that He is the one that gives to us. The word "remember" means "to have profound respect, to recount, and to be mindful." Our minds must note that God Almighty is the one Who has provided. We must always **acknowledge that it is GOD** Who has given us this power to acquire wealth.

He gives us the **power** to get wealth. He is the one Who has given us the ability. He gives to us, that we may use it. He expects us to use it.

There is a reason that He gives us the power to be wealthy.

He wants us to be wealthy, to fulfill His **covenant**. His covenant is His promise that He loves all! His covenant is that if we will come to Him with a repentant heart, He forgives and will save.

> God wants us wealthy so we can fulfill His covenant

He **swore** His covenant! When a person makes a promise, covenant, they make it to someone 'above or greater' than they. God is the greatest, therefore He swore it to Himself, because there isn't one greater than He.

GOD WANTS YOU TO CARE FOR THE ORPHANS AND THE WIDOWS.

> *"He who has pity on the poor lends to the Lord, and He will pay back what he has given."*
>
> PROV 19:17

This verse is saying that we are **lending** to the Lord! How can this be? How can I say that I have loaned to God and now He is my debtor? We must not forget that God already owns all that we have. The Word says, "The earth is the Lord's and the fullness thereof." All we have or seemingly own belongs to God!

So if I help the poor, then I'm not only lending to the Lord, but I have placed myself in a position of trusting God to care for me. There's a sense that God becomes a debtor. Now, don't shut me down. God is a debtor to Himself to be the keeper of His own Word! "When God made his promise to Abraham, since there was no one greater for him to swear by, he swore by himself "(Heb 6:13 NIV). If I place my trust in God, then He is bound to His own word and honor to uphold His Word.

So, we don't really "lend" to God in helping the poor. We place ourselves in a position that God will bless us!

James 1:27 says it like this:

> *"Pure and undefiled religion before God and the Father is this: to visit orphans and widows in their trouble, and to keep oneself unspotted from the world."*

Orphans are children whose parents are not in the child's life, for whatever reason, and widows are women whose husbands have died. Husbands and fathers play such an irreplaceable role in the family, that God Himself says that He will be a father to the fatherless.

We shouldn't view caring for widows and orphans simply as a command from God, but there is such a blessing when we do care for them. We need to remember that we ALL were adopted into God's family through Christ.

Helping the widows, orphans, and those in need is an example of Christ's love.

GOD WANTS YOU TO BE THE HEAD AND NOT THE TAIL.

"And all people of the earth shall see that you are called by the name [and in the presence of] the Lord, and they shall be afraid of you. And **the Lord shall make you have a surplus of prosperity**, *through the fruit of your body, of your livestock, and of your ground, in the land which the Lord swore to your fathers to give you. The Lord shall open to you His good treasury, the heavens, to give the rain of your land in its season and* **to bless all the work of your hands**; *and you shall lend to many nations, but you shall not borrow. And* **the Lord shall make you the head, and not the tail; and you shall be above only, and you shall not be beneath,** *if you heed the commandments of the Lord your God which I command you this day and are watchful to do them."*

DEUT 28:10-13 AMP, EMPHASIS ADDED

So, what does it mean to be the head? The Hebrew word "head" means "to lead as the head of an army." God's leadership and ability in us makes others want to follow us, because of Him within us! He is saying **all** the people, not just our family members, or neighbors, but all. Everyone you come in contact with will take notice that you are called by name.

You can walk in every situation with the boldness of God.

You will have a surplus of prosperity.

It doesn't say that He will give you a surplus of poverty. He says that He will give you a surplus, and abundant prosperity.

He will bless the work of your hands! We need to keep our hands busy!

He can't bless what we aren't doing.

I've talked with many people who want the blessings of God and desire to live in prosperity, but they aren't working. They are receiving government assistance, they don't have a job, they aren't looking for a job ... and yet they want God to prosper them. Beloved, God can't bless us if we aren't putting our hands to work and obeying the Scriptures. God blesses the work of our hands, so we need to work. In fact, that was the first instruction He gave to Adam and Eve. He told them to tend the garden. He gave them a job to do. Work wasn't under the curse. Work is part of the blessing!

We must cooperate with God and His Word.

Remember, we are instructed to:

> ***"Heed the commandments of the Lord your God,** which I command you this day!"*
>
> DUET 28:13

Everyday we should look for His instruction, His commandment, so that we can walk in the prosperous life He desires for us!

CHAPTER 2

The 10% Factor

As Christians, we have a source of financial abundance that is limitless. What is this source, or rather, who is this source? God! God is limitless! And He has promised to meet all of our needs according to HIS riches in glory! This includes spiritual, physical, and material needs. Some of the most prosperous people of all time, were men and women of God—Abraham, Solomon, Esther, Ruth and more. God wants all of us to prosper, but in order to receive financially from God, He wants us to fulfill certain responsibilities. If we do our part, then God says He will fulfill His part and meet all of our needs. This is where we have responsibility and authority to become prosperous.

The Bible has a lot to say about prosperity and money. In fact, there are over 2,500 scriptures concerning money!

Jesus talked more about money than He did heaven or hell. Because Jesus talked a lot about money, then it must be important to us. He wants us to build wealth and one of the greatest ways that we can build wealth, is by tithing first. This is the 10% factor!

There has been a great controversy in the body of Christ when it comes to the tithe. Many have disagreed with tithing for today, because they say the tithe occurred under the Law, and now we are under grace so we don't need to tithe. Some will say that God doesn't require us to tithe today, because of this grace.

Let's begin with the Old Testament. We see that tithing did occur under the Law:

> *"And all the tithe of the land, **whether** of the seed of the land or of the fruit of the tree, **is** the Lord's. It **is** holy to the Lord. If a man wants at all to redeem any of his tithes, he shall add one-fifth to it. And concerning the tithe of the herd or the flock, of whatever passes under the rod, the tenth one shall be holy to the Lord."*
>
> LEV 27:30-32 NKJV, EMPHASIS ADDED

We see that Moses came to the conclusion that a tithing system was necessary for the nation of Israel. This occurred at the beginning of the second year of the Exodus. He told the Israelites that they should give a tenth part of their seed crops and fruit trees plus every tenth animal to the treasury in the newly erected Tabernacle.

Proverbs 3:9 states, *"Honor the Lord with your possessions, and with the firstfruits of all your increase."* Tithing was part of the Law, but we must realize that tithing occurred even before the Law.

In the Old Testament Abraham tithed to Melchizedek before the Law was instituted:

*"For this Melchizedek, king of Salem, priest of the Most High God, who met Abraham returning from the slaughter of the kings and blessed him, to whom also Abraham gave a tenth part of all, first being translated 'king of righteousness,' and then also king of Salem, meaning 'king of peace,' without father, without mother, without genealogy, having neither beginning of days nor end of life, but made like the Son of God, remains a priest continually. Now consider how great this man **was**, to whom even the patriarch Abraham gave a tenth of the spoils."*

HEB 7:1-4 NKJV, EMPHASIS ADDED

The tenth of the spoils was the tithe! This occurred about 500 years **before** the Law. Abraham tithed to Melchizedek, the High Priest before the Law, out of honor.

Who was Melchizedek? The word Melichizedek comes from two Hebrew words, melek and tsedeq. The Word melek means "king" and tsedeq means "righteousness." A king was preeminent in his jurisdiction, so he has to be preeminent in righteousness. He was not only the High Priest but he was also the king of Salem. The word Salem in the Hebrew means "peace." Melchizedek was the king of Peace.

Abraham honored Melchizedek; therefore, Melchizedek honored and blessed Abraham.

As we honor the Lord, He honors us.

Now some may be thinking that this occurred in the Old Testament to the High Priest, so why would I need to tithe today? Because the tithe, was not only under the law, but occurred before the law. Our spiritual father, Abraham, tithed to the High Priest 500 years before the law! Do we have one today? Do we have a High Priest today?

We do have a High Priest today!

Because he had no father and no mother and was without genealogy, most theologians agree that Melchizedek was a type of Christ.

Who is our High Priest today?

> *"Therefore, holy brethren, partakers of the heavenly calling, consider the Apostle and High Priest of our confession, Christ Jesus."*
>
> HEB 3:1 NKJV

Jesus Christ is not only our High Priest, but He also receives our tithe today.

> *"Here mortal men receive tithes, but there he **receives them**, of whom it is witnessed that he lives."*
>
> HEB 7:8 NKJV

The mortal men this scripture is speaking of are God's ministers on earth and Jesus receives our tithe personally and places them on the altar of God! Karen, are you saying that I have a High Priest who receives my tithe, even today? YES!

It's more than placing a check in a tithe envelope.

Ministers of God may receive our actual tithe money, but it is the Lord receiving our obedience. We are tithing to the Lord. The tithe is consecrated to the Lord for His service, for the advancement of His kingdom on the earth.

This brings us to the New Testament and what it says about tithing. See, we are no longer under the law, but under grace.

> *"... for you are not under law but under grace ..."*
>
> ROMANS 6:14 NKJV

How much greater can we give because we are under grace?

We aren't giving our tithe because we are under the Law or because God says so, we are able to give our tithe because we are operating and under grace.

If I told you that Jesus Himself instructs us to tithe, would you tithe?

Jesus Himself instructs us to tithe.

> *"Woe to you, scribes and Pharisees, hypocrites! For you pay tithe of mint and anise and cummin, and have neglected the weightier **matters** of the law: justice and mercy and faith. These you ought to have done, without leaving the others undone."*
>
> MATT 23:23 NKJV

Jesus is saying to the religious folks, Pharisees, to tithe. They were so religious in attempting to keep the Law that they tithed not only on the food they were going to eat, but also the spices they were going to place on their food. This seems to be way overboard to tithe even on spices, but Jesus validates what they are doing. He didn't stop there though, He says they neglected the weightier matters of the law: justice, mercy and faith. Being just, showing mercy and having faith were certainly weightier and more important, but Jesus is saying not to neglect tithing. Justice is doing the right thing, so when we tithe, we are doing the right thing.

Jesus is saying not to stop tithing.

> "...These you ought to have done, without leaving the others undone."
>
> MATT 23:23 NKJV

Returning the tithe to God causes us to remember that He is the owner of all things.

> "The earth is the Lords and all it's fullness."
>
> PSALM 24:1

> "You shall remember the Lord your God, for it is He who gives you power to get wealth."
>
> DEUT 8:18 NKJV

It is the Lord who owns it all! Everything we seemingly own is really on loan. We are but stewards, God owns it all. We are honoring Him when we return the tithe to Him!

When we tithe, we are **honoring** the Lord because we recognize He owns it all and He is the one that gives us the power to get wealth.

> "A son honors his father and a servant his master. If I then am your father where is My honor? If I am a master where is my reverence?"
>
> (MAL 1:6 NKJV).

The word "honor" means, "to value, see as weighty and precious."

Webster's dictionary defines honor as, "to revere, to respect; to treat with submission."

God isn't an ego-maniac. He isn't up in heaven demanding that He receive honor. God is worthy of all honor because He is God.

We see in this verse that submission to authority is true honor. To say we honor authority while holding back from submission and obedience to it, is to deceive ourselves.

> *"But be doers of the word, and not hearers only, deceiving yourselves."*
>
> JAMES 1:22 NKJV

When we hear the truth and know the truth, but we refuse to walk in it and obey, we deceive ourselves!

We can't say we honor the Lord and not submit to His will.

We can't say we honor the Lord and not submit to His way.

We can't say we honor the Lord and not tithe.

To honor authority is to submit to authority and we dishonor authority by not submitting to it.

When we don't tithe, we are not submitting to God nor honoring Him.

God doesn't want honor by legalism or law, but from a son or a daughter's heart to a father. When we bring our tithe into the storehouse, we are honoring our Father because He has designated that 10% for a divine purpose.

Those of us who are parents want our children to obey us because we know what's best for our children, and want them to walk in the best. We want them to have the best!

We want them to obey us because we see ahead!

God, as our Father, wants what's best for us—His children so He prepared the plan of tithing that will bring the best for us. He sees ahead!

When we tithe, we bring honor to our Father.

> *"If you be willing and obedient, you will eat the good of the land."*
>
> IS 1:19 NKJV

This scripture doesn't say if we are **willing** we will eat the good of the land. It's not enough that we are willing to tithe and not do it.

We must be **willing and obedient** by doing it, then we will eat the good of the land.

Obedience and honor brought the blessing!

We understand that we honor God by tithing, so **how** do we tithe?

> *"Bring the whole tithe into the storehouse, that there may be meat in my house."*
>
> MAL 3:10

There's a specific amount to be brought to a designated place for a particular purpose.

We see that the tithe is an amount of 10%.

The word tithe means 10, therefore the tithe is 10% of our income.

We can't negotiate the tithe. Some have said, "I tithe 3% of my income to God." 3% isn't the tithe. 5% isn't the tithe.

The tithe is 10%, and it's a set amount.

Some folks may say, "I pay my bills and save some and then when I get ready to tithe, I don't have it."

That's upside down. We need to turn that right-side up.

When we get paid, we need to tithe **first,** then pay our bills and then save some.

When we receive our paycheck, and pay bills and use the tithe to pay our mortgage payment, the mortgage company doesn't have the power or ability to bless our finances.

When we receive our paycheck and use the tithe at the mall, the mall doesn't have the power or ability to bless our finances. When we use the tithe to pay the car payment, the car dealership doesn't have the power to bless our finances.

But when we get paid and tithe to our local church first, God has the power and ability to bless our finances. And He will!

In the early days when I first got saved, I struggled greatly in this area. I had a job and I tithed, but I wondered if it would work. My pay didn't change. I had a set amount of pay that I would receive every two weeks, regardless if I worked overtime or not. So, I didn't have the opportunity to make more money with working overtime. I would fight thoughts that if I tithed, I would have less. I mean, if I give 10% to God, then I have 10% less to pay my bills. How could this possibly work?

I began to tithe anyway, even though I didn't completely understand the tithing concept. I did this out of obedience to God's Word.

As a result, I began to see God work in ways I never thought would happen. I would receive a bonus at work, which never happened. I would buy groceries and get such great deals that I didn't even have to spend the amount of money I had allotted for groceries. Things began to happen that caused me to believe that the tithe works! Dr. John Polis says, "Obeying God, even without fully understanding, will result in His blessings!" God blesses our obedience!

We see that the tithe is a set amount to be brought to a designated **place**. Where is this place?

*"Bring all the tithe into the **storehouse**"*

MAL 3:10

The storehouse represents the local church. This is the place where you come to worship, get fed the Word of God, and to be cared for.

Some folks say that they tithe 10%, but they divide it up and they place 2% here, 5% there, and the remaining 3% somewhere else. The tithe is 10% but it's to be placed in one location!

God has designed the tithe to be placed in the local church.

If you're dividing your tithe up, you should ask yourself if these other places pray for you?

Do they care for you?

Do they watch over your soul?

The tithe is to be placed in the local church where you are getting prayed for, cared for, and where the pastor and elders watch over your soul!

We see that the amount is 10%, and the place is the local church, and now we can see the purpose of the tithe.

The tithe was designated for the **purpose** to provide resources for the Levitical priesthood.

According to the book of Numbers, it was designated so the priests wouldn't have to work secularly.

> *"Behold, I have given the children of Levi all the tithes in Israel as an inheritance in return for the work which they perform, the work of the tabernacle of meeting."*
>
> NUM 18:21 NKJV

Today, the purpose is to ensure that there is meat in the house; that the ministry locally can continue.

The tithe causes there to be food in the house, which is revelation knowledge. When we tithe in faith, God reveals His wisdom to us.

The set leader of the church you are placed in has been designated as the pasture where you are to be fed.

> *"He makes me to lie down in green pastures; He leads me beside the still waters."*
>
> PS 23:2 NKJV

When God places you in a local church, that is the place He is going to feed you. The shepherd (pastor) is going to feed you the Word of God that you need to hear. This is the place, the green pasture where you can eat and grow. Have you ever been in the service and the pastor is speaking and it's exactly what you need to hear? This is the place where you are going to get fed!

Throughout Scripture, the tithe was indicative of Israel's spiritual condition. The tithe is a warfare weapon!

When Israel tithed, they were winning wars and doing well. When they weren't tithing, it meant they were losing wars.

God doesn't want His people to lose or not do well. He wants you to win and come out on top! He wants you to succeed in everything you do!

In Malachi 3, God says that He will rebuke the devourer for our sakes so the enemy doesn't destroy the fruit of our ground.

God is saying that He will take care of our enemy.

I've known some people that work and they work really hard, but it never is enough, because things will break, or cars need repaired often, or there is something that always seems to happen to them which causes the "fruit" in their life to be destroyed. It seems they can never get ahead.

This depicts a person who isn't tithing and honoring the Lord.

> *"So that he will not destroy the fruit of your ground, nor shall the vine fail to bear fruit for you in the field."*
>
> MAL 3:11 NKJV

God is saying that if you will obey and tithe, He will ensure that your fruit will remain and He will rebuke the devourer in your life!

Fruit is what is produced from what is planted. When you have production in your life, you don't want to see it die, wither, or have the fruit destroyed. Everything your life represents can be prosperous, producing, and remain. This is the fruit that God doesn't want to wither or be destroyed. Your family life, your relationships, your workplace, and your finances can all be producing and prosperous when you tithe!

> Everything in your life can be prosperous, producing, and remain

He promises that He will rebuke the devourer.

So when the enemy comes and tries to make your new car break down, or your washing machine quit, God will rebuke (stop) the enemy from stealing in your life.

Let me encourage you: if you're not tithing presently, begin to obey the Word of God and watch God move on your behalf. Watch as your finances get into order. He will rebuke the devourer and you'll become a delightsome land—a land that is always producing.

CHAPTER 3

How Did We Get Into Debt?

This is a valid question. To understand debt, we must first look at the history of debt.

According to the Federal Reserve Bank of New York, "Americans have now borrowed more money than they had at the height of the credit bubble in 2008, just as the global financial system began to collapse. Since World War II, total household debt had been increasing, with only a few interruptions. The financial crisis changed that steady upward march. In late 2008, household debt began a decline that would last for 19 consecutive quarters, an unprecedented period of deleveraging during which many Americans shied away from new borrowing. Total debt began to rise again in 2013, finally hitting a new high in this year's first quarter. Students have gone deep into debt in the belief that a college degree will eventually lead to a higher income. But many students have graduated into a job market where wages have been rising slowly, leaving them with more debt than they can pay off. Economists are now unsure about how this mountain of student debt will affect the broader economy. Unlike mortgages, student loans cannot typically be shed or restructured, which means that more Americans are shouldering a type of debt that could weigh them down for the rest of their lives, preventing them from buying homes or starting businesses" (*The New York Times, Federal Reserve Bank, 2017*).

Some folks have wondered if debt is bad and if so, what can we do about it?

It's reported that 63% of Americans are one paycheck away from financial disaster and can't deal with a $400 emergency. This is astounding! If you went home right now and found that your hot water tank needed to be replaced, could you take care of it with money in the bank or would you have to go into debt?

How do we deal with debt in an environment where almost everyone has themself in debt? We need to look into God's Word!

What does the Bible say about debt? Am I thinking the way God thinks?

1. Is debt prohibited in the Bible?

No, it is not! No where does it say, "you cannot go into debt." The Word doesn't say that you can't have debt, but it does mention principles and practices we should heed regarding debt.

> *"The rich rules over the poor, And the borrower is servant to the lender."*
>
> PROV 22:7 NKJV

Solomon wrote this verse, but debt wasn't as prevalent then as it is today. We see in this verse, that when we are in debt, we become a slave to those that we have borrowed from. We become a servant to the mortgage company, the credit card company and any other place or person that we owe.

2. **The absence of debt is praised!**

    Moses made it clear that God had promised the people that when they obeyed, they would be blessed for their work. They would be lenders, instead of borrowers.

    "The Lord will open the heavens, the storehouse of his bounty, to send rain on your land in season and to bless all the work of your hands. You will lend to many nations but will borrow from none."

    DEUT 28:12 NIV

    God is showing us that we are the head and not the tail, because we are lenders and not borrowers. When you're the head, you are out in front; you're ahead of everyone else. You're not coming in last place, you're in first place!

3. **It doesn't say that debt is an exercise of faith!**

    If we say that we are using our faith by borrowing money, then are we saying that God **needs** us to use a lender to meet our needs? Don't put a lending company in place of God!

4. **The Word doesn't say that God will bail you out of debt.**

    Some folks have the mindset that they can spend and spend, because God has promised to get them out of their problems. According to Philippians 4:19, God will meet all of your needs, but He didn't say He would cancel the consequences of unwise behavior. I'm not saying that if you're in debt that God won't help you. I'm saying we can't continue to go into debt needlessly and expect God to just "fix it."

5. **God instructs us on lending and borrowing!**

   a. We are instructed to not become usury. What is usury? It is the amount paid for the use of money; hence interest.

   "If you lend money to one of my people among who is needy, do not treat it like a business deal; charge no interest."

   EX 22:25 NIV

   b. Vows must be honored.

   "The wicked borrows and does not pay back, but the righteous is gracious and gives"

   PS. 37:21 NASB

   If we have debt, we must pay it back.

   c. Limits are placed on collateral.

   "When you make a loan of any kind to your neighbor, do not go into their house to get what is offered to you as a pledge. Stay outside and let the neighbor to whom you are making the loan bring the pledge out to you."

   DEUT 24:10-11 NIV

6. **God teaches us about the dangers of debt.**

   According to Proverbs 22:7, the borrower is servant to the lender.

   So, we see that there are some dangers with debt that we need to consider.

   a. Debt reveals our motives.

We should ask ourselves, do we desire to go into debt because of a lack of satisfaction with what God has provided? Do we take the opportunity to acquire debt because we aren't willing to delay gratification? Are we impatient? Maturity is being willing and able to wait!

Lending institutions often play to our weaknesses. If we aren't watchful, we can skirt from God's principles and call our debt 'good business.'

b. Debt forces you to trade off!

If you go into debt, the Bible teaches that you must be faithful to pay it. Because debts must be paid, other priorities are forced to go into second place.

c. Debt can hinder your generosity!

If you're in debt and there is a need that needs met in someone's life, you may not be able to assist them, because you're obligated to pay your debts.

If God is more than enough, then should we borrow? Are we putting our trust in credit cards and the ability to go into debt, rather than including God in our decisions? Can we trust God to supply and provide for us in the area of finances?

Is debt a salvation issue? No, but the Bible does have some things to say about debt:

> "The rich rule over the poor and the borrower is slave to the lender."
>
> PROV 22:7 NIV

So, it's not a salvation issue, but this verse does explain that we become slaves when we have debt. So how do we get out of debt? What are the goals that we need to attain along the way to get to our debt free destination?

What are the reasons people go into debt? I have come up with some reasons that may surprise you. Check your answers as well, and be truthful with yourself. We can't change what we don't acknowledge.

1. **Same expenses, but have the same income**

    Have you heard the saying that we spend according to our income? When our income increases, our spending increases! The problem is, when our income drops, we don't always adjust the expenses. This is where we can get into trouble. It's imperative that the expenses drop when the income drops. The sooner adjustments are made, the better!

2. **Poor money management**

    So many people don't have a monthly budget. The folks that don't have a budget are ones who wonder at the end of the month where the money went. Writing a budget each and every month is a must! If you don't budget, then you don't know where your money is going and the key to paying off debt and building wealth, is being in control and aware of expenses. A budget puts you in control of your money. You might be spending money each month unnecessarily. Planning doesn't have to be difficult. It's a matter of writing down your income and expenses and following the plan.

3. **Un-employment**

    Some folks that get laid-off from their job begin to have the mindset that it's temporary. It may be, but let's adjust our expenses accordingly. What if the job doesn't call you back to work for 6 months? Do you have an emergency fund to cover your expenses during this period of time? Get the expenses in line with the current income.

4. **Gambling**

    Some consider this an entertainment. Unfortunately, this is rather expensive. Besides, if God wanted you to win, wouldn't He give you the winning numbers? If you're participating in this, see your pastor or counselor and get help!

    Every lottery ticket or areas you're gambling, will rob your future!

5. **Saving very little**

    The best way to plan for unexpected expenses is to plan for them. I had someone tell me that they felt that planning for unexpected events was a lack of faith. I find that going into debt is far more a lack of faith than being prepared. Save up to 6 months of living expenses in a separate account marked for emergencies. Then when emergencies arise, it doesn't become stressful because you have the money set aside to take care of it. I don't know anyone that has regretted having a savings account.

6. **No communication about money**

    If you're married, communicate with your spouse regarding finances. Keep the lines of communication open and set up a strategy. Most couples are opposites, so one may be a spender and the other a saver. That's ok that you're opposites! What's important is that you set up goals together that you agree upon and then move towards those goals together! Promise to be honest with each other and lay it all out on the table.

7. **Financially illiterate**

    There are some people that don't have any idea how money works, save, or even balance a checkbook. It's not too late to learn. Get with a financial advisor, your pastor, a financial coach and begin learning. Financial mistakes are expensive. Get educated and get in control.

8. **Apathy**

Some people have the attitude and mindset that they just don't care. This is irresponsible behavior, because God has entrusted you with your job, and desires that you be a good steward with what he has entrusted you with. Would you give your children more electronics if they don't take care of what they have? The Scripture says, "Know well the state of your flocks." We are to be aware of what we have, care for it and know our financial state.

Most people I have coached have acquired credit card debt. But to understand how we have credit card debt, we need to understand the history of credit cards.

Credit cards are issued to individuals to allow them to pay a merchant for goods based on the individual's promise to pay the card issuer. The card issuer, usually a bank, creates a revolving account and permits a line of credit to the cardholder. Credit cards combine payment services with extensions of credit.

Bank issued cards came on the scene in 1946, when John Biggins, a Brooklyn bank started the "Charg-It" card. The bank would pay the stores and be responsible for collecting the debt from the card-holders.

Biggins' idea was implemented on a small scale—only available for residents and merchants within a few blocks of the bank, but the idea caught on quickly.

Four years later, the Diners Club Card was instituted by Frank McNamara.

McNamara came up with this idea when a year earlier, had forgot his wallet while attending a dinner in New York.

By 1951, Diners Club had 20,000 cardholders.

The American Express card launched in 1958, and expanded it's territory to other countries. By 1964, 1 million American Express cards were in use.

Later, major banks would create their own consumer cards, but instead of having to pay their bill each month, bank cards would truly become "credit cards" by offering revolving credit. This allowed the cardholders to carry their monthly balance forward for a fee. This is where the real trouble began. Most folks do not pay off their credit card each month. If you do, you're one of very few.

Bank of America was launched in 1958, and by 1966 Bank Americard became the nation's first general purpose credit card. It was renamed Visa ten years later.

According to the Federal Reserve data, 70% of Americans have at least one credit card. This means that there are about 174 million American adults with at least one credit card!

Total U.S. outstanding revolving debt, was $953.3 billion as of May 2017.

We see the history of how Americans have spiraled into debt. But we can't spiral out of debt. Larry Burkett says, "You can slip into debt, but you can't slip out of debt."

> "You can slip into debt, but you can't slip out of debt."
>
> —LARRY BURKETT

CHAPTER 4

Help, I'm Overwhelmed!

I have coached many folks in the area of finances, and they all have one thing in common—STRESS!

Being overextended in the money arena can certainly cause a person to feel overwhelmed.

Over several years, I have found some habits folks have that may indicate the reason for their debt and stress. If you find yourself engaging in any of these habits, you may want to consider changing them.

1. **Bills are on automatic pay**

    Now, some folks may argue the fact that this saves them time, but in the long run this can cost you dearly. You may not forget to make that payment each month, but paying bills automatically takes you out of the process. When the money comes out of your account, this can be disastrous if you live on the edge of not having enough money in your account.

2. **Spending more than you earn**

   Living beyond your means will lead to trouble. If you have to reach for plastic to make it through the month, this is a huge red flag. This includes charging necessities, carrying balances and then transferring credit card balances.

3. **Paying late**

   If you don't have financial problems, but you end up paying your payments late, this will trigger financial problems. You'll end up being charged late fees and it will go against your credit.

4. **Home Equity loans**

   A HELOC, Home Equity Line of Credit, operates like the ultimate line of credit, allowing you to buy what you need even at a low interest rate. If you miss a payment on a credit card, you get a bad mark, but if you miss a payment on your HELOC, you're putting your house at risk.

5. **Co-signing a loan**

   Think about this! When you co-sign a loan, you're generally co-signing for someone you know. It could be a friend or relative. This can make for a very interesting Thanksgiving dinner, especially if the person you're co-signing for doesn't pay. Their missed or late payments will go against you. The bank is requiring them to have a co-signer on their loan because they don't trust them to pay them back.

6. **Having no budget**

   If you don't have a budget, it makes it difficult to define where your money is going on a monthly basis. A budget puts you in control of your money. If you're not budgeting, you're most likely experiencing a lot of stress.

People want to get rid of the stress, and one of the ways to do this is to get your finances under control. The reason they aren't under control is because they're out of control. If you won't control your money, your money will be out of control!

So, how do we do this? How do we get our money under control?

We must look to change in these 3 areas:

- MIND
- MOUTH
- MAKE

MIND

Let's begin with the mind.

> *"For as he thinks in his heart, so is he."*
>
> PROV. 23:7 NKJV

This means that whatever we are thinking on is what we are!

WHAT?

Yes, it's imperative that we take notice of what we are thinking. What we think is what we become!

> *"And do not be conformed to this world, but be transformed by the renewing of your mind, that you may prove what **is** that good and acceptable and perfect will of God."*
>
> ROM 12:2 NKJV

This verse is telling us to "**shun the mold**." We aren't to be conformed to this world. We must renew our mind.

The word "conformed" means to conform to the same pattern, to fashion or to shape." It means "to mold." We aren't to allow ourselves to be squeezed into the world's mold.

When we allow ourselves to be shaped, fashioned into the world's mold, we begin to think like the world, act like the world, and be like the world.

We are to "**shape our mind**." This verse tells us to "be transformed by the renewing of your mind." The word transform is the Greek word "metamorphoo" where we get the word "metamorphosis." This describes a complete transformation, just like a caterpillar is transformed into a butterfly. See, the caterpillar "becomes" the butterfly through this process.

We are changed when we renew our minds to the Word of God.

We become something different.

When God saved you, your spirit man was born-again, but we must renew our minds to His Word, His Will, and His Work.

What is that?

God desires us to be prosperous!

> "Beloved, I pray that you may prosper in all things and be in health, just as your soul prospers."
>
> 3 JOHN 2 NKJV

When our mind is changed and brought under the power of God, our soul can be brought under control.

We must fill ourselves with the Word of God. We must think on the Word of God.

*"Finally, brethren, whatever things are true, whatever things **are** noble, whatever things **are** just, whatever things **are** pure, whatever things **are** lovely, whatever things **are** of good report, if **there** is any virtue and if **there is** anything praiseworthy—meditate on these things."*

PHIL 4:8 NKJV, EMPHASIS ADDED

Now some may be thinking, "But I am not being truthful when I am behind on my bills and can't pay them, yet I say I can pay them."

I understand that may be a fact, but truth, which is God's Word, overrides facts.

Begin thinking thoughts "I am able to pay all my bills each month because God's Word says that I can."

> The truth (God's Word) overrides facts

Stop saying things like, "I am in debt, I'm in debt up to my eyeballs."

Whatever you think on, you will move towards.

Let me say that again, whatever you think on, you will move towards.

Begin saying, "I am debt free!"

Make a list of Scriptures that back up what you are believing and begin to speak them aloud every day. If you want to become debt free, then have Scriptures to back it up. You're not creating anything unless you're saying something.

We are made in the image of God. God created the world with words!

This verse in Philippians also says to think on things that are a "good report." A good report is "reputable, well spoken of." Begin speaking the "good report" over your finances.

If you think, I can't pay my bills, you will move towards that.

Wouldn't it be better to think and speak that you are able to pay all your bills?

Say this: "I am out of debt, and all my needs are met and I have abundance and never lack."

Say that over and over again and you will begin to believe it.

"As a man thinketh in his heart so is he."

Whatever you think on is what you will become.

Whatever you think on is what you will move towards.

Someone once said, "Expectation is the atmosphere for miracles."

Think about David and Goliath. David was a youngest of his brothers but expected that he was going to take that giant Goliath down. In fact, he said it before he saw it happen.

> *"This day the Lord will deliver you into my hand, and I will strike you and take your head from you. And this day I will give the carcasses of the camp of the Philistines to the birds of the air and the wild beasts of the earth, that all the earth may know that there is a God in Israel. Then all this assembly shall know that the Lord does not save with sword and spear; for the battle is the Lord's, and He will give you into our hands"*
>
> 1 SAM 17:46-47 NKJV

David first thought it, then said what was going to happen, and then did it. He still had to take action and move towards Goliath. He still had to aim and throw the stone at Goliath, but he said it before it happened.

What are you thinking about in the area of your finances? Begin to speak this out. What will you begin to speak over your finances? What action will you take to create what you speak?

We not only need to think with our minds, we must speak with our mouths.

MOUTH

Words are powerful!

> *"Death and life **are** in the power of the tongue, And those who love it will eat its fruit."*
>
> PROV 18:21 NKJV, EMPHASIS ADDED

> *"Indeed, we put bits in horses' mouths that they may obey us, and we turn their whole body. Look also at ships: although they are so large and are driven by fierce winds, they are turned by a very small rudder wherever the pilot desires. Even so the tongue is a little member and boasts great things. See how great a forest a little fire kindles."*
>
> JAMES 3:3-5 NKJV

We see in both of these verses that words will produce what we say!

I think of a large ship that is going out to sea, and what will turn that ship is the small rudder. It is amazing that something so small can move such a large object.

Your finances may not be going in the right direction. You may even be in debt so far that you don't see a way out. One powerful way to help turn your finances around is to speak words that will help turn you in the right direction.

Now with the ship, although the rudder is turning the direction, there are still workers manning the vessel. We must continue to work, pay our bills, and manage our money in a greater way while we are speaking words to turn our financial situation around.

Declare Psalm 35:27—

"God delights in the prosperity of His servant, therefore, I declare I am out of debt and all my needs are met."

Declare this—

According to 2 Cor. 9:7, I am a cheerful giver, and I will sow as the Holy Spirit directs me.

Now say—

According to Ps. 103:20, I command angels to go and bring my promotion and increase.

This was an area in which I struggled for years. I would think about all the bills I had, and how much income I had, and the lack of income to pay the bills; therefore, I ended up speaking what I was thinking. When I finally got the revelation that I needed to think according to God's Word, I began to see a change in my mind and in my mouth.

I changed my mind so I would think wealth, overflow, abundance, and prosperity. This resulted in my speaking that which I was thinking. Words are powerful and they are a result of what we think upon and believe. What do you believe about your finances? Because what you truly believe is what you will speak! If you want to change your financial situation, begin to think and mediate upon God's Word and speak it forth into existence!

MAKE

This brings me to the third point. We have discussed that we need to keep our minds, our thoughts, in accordance to God's Word. We need to ensure that our mouth, like a small rudder of a ship, will help turn our finances in the right direction. Now, we need to look at what we make. What are we doing?

It's so important that we get our minds and our mouths in line with God's Word, but we also need to **DO and apply what we believe!**

> *"But be ye doers of the word, and not hearers only, deceiving your own selves. For if any be a hearer of the word, and not a doer, he is like unto a man beholding his natural face in a glass: For he beholdeth himself, and goeth his way, and straightway forgetteth what manner of man he was."*
>
> JAMES 1:22-24 NKJV

See, we open ourselves up to deception when we aren't doers of the Word. We will do what we believe. So if we are saying that we are out of debt, yet we still purchase on credit, then we aren't applying and doing according to what we are speaking.

We do what we believe.

> *"Thus also faith by itself, if it does not have works, is dead."*
>
> JAMES 2 :17 NKJV

People act in line with what they believe. For example, if we believe that a stove is hot, we won't place our hand on it. If we believe that exercise is good for us to maintain our bodies, we will exercise. If we believe that debt isn't a good idea, then we won't go into debt. If we truly believe God is who He says He is and that the Bible means what it says, we will act accordingly.

Let's look at an example in the Word of God!

> *"A certain woman of the wives of the sons of the prophets cried out to Elisha, saying, "Your servant my husband is dead, and you know that your servant feared the Lord. And the creditor is coming to take my two sons to be his slaves." So Elisha said to her, "What shall I do for you? Tell me, what do you have in the house?" And she said, "Your maidservant has nothing in the house but a jar of oil."*
> *Then he said, "Go, borrow vessels from everywhere, from all your neighbors—empty vessels; do not gather just a few. And when you have come in, you shall shut the door behind you and your sons; then pour it into all those vessels, and set aside the full ones." So she went from him and shut the door behind her and her sons, who brought the vessels to her; and she poured it out. Now it came to pass, when the vessels were full, that she said to her son, "Bring me another vessel." And he said to her, "There is not another vessel." So the oil ceased. Then she came and told the man of God. And he said, "Go, sell the oil and pay your debt; and you and your sons live on the rest."*
>
> 2 KINGS 4:1-7 NKJV

The widow did and acted because she believed. Notice that the woman did what the prophet instructed. She used her faith in what the man of

God said and did it! Her faith was being stretched. When you make up your mind to live a debt-free life, it will take faith and action!

God expanded her faith **personally, publicly,** and **privately.**

Elisha asked her what she had in the house. Although it didn't look like she had much, it revealed she had oil. At times, it seems our problems are so large, and our possessions are so small. But when God makes a promise, we can guarantee that He will make it good He meets our needs and builds our faith personally.

God will also expand our faith publicly. She was told to go to her neighbors and borrow vessels. I wonder what her neighbors thought? God used her to speak not only to herself by publicly sending her to her neighbors, but I am sure it spoke to her neighbors. This is faith in action! This is faith that can be seen—it's public!

God will also expand your faith privately. She went back into her house, after gathering all those vessels and shut the door. Now her faith was private. She began to pour oil into all those empty vessels and as she did, the supply was increased!

What is God asking you to do? What measures are you willing to take to allow the Lord to expand your faith personally, publicly, and privately?

God will expand
your faith
personally, publicly,
and privately

CHAPTER 5

Debt Demolition

Being in debt can be stressful to say the least. No matter what your circumstance, if you have debt, you are obligated to pay it back.

Sometimes debt is the result of overspending—simply buying things beyond your means. It can often happen as an unintended consequence of too much holiday spending. Whatever the reason you find yourself in debt, let me encourage you: people are getting out of debt every single day, and they are doing this in a short period of time. How do they do this? The answer is simple, they have a plan!

Planning is a key ingredient when you're determined to demolish debt!

Let's look at goal-setting first. I heard someone say that when setting goals we must do it the SMART way. Using the acrostic, S.M.A.R.T, let's define it.

- **Specific**—When we set goals they must be specific. We may consider having a goal to get out of debt. Certainly this is a good goal, but it must be more specific. It could be better with, "I will pay off debt in the amount of $123,425."
- **Measurabl**e—Use precise amounts, but also add a date to that amount. "I will pay off $123,425 by May 15, 2020." This enables you to check and measure your success.
- **Attainable**—The goal should be attainable. Can you pay that off in 2 years? Look at the goal and see if it is realistic. If the goal is a pipe dream, you will become discouraged and stop trying. It should stretch you, but be within reach.
- **Relevant**—Is the goal relevant to your life? You must answer why this goal is important to you. Why do you want to be out of doubt? How will this change your life? Goals that are relevant carry the weight of motivation behind them.
- **Timely**—Set a target date for you to reach your goal. Work backwards and set several markers along the way to help you know whether you are on track, behind, or ahead of schedule so you can make the appropriate adjustments and hit your target.

More steps on building wealth will be discussed in a later chapter, but before you can build you need to be free. First we must look at debt demolition.

When it comes to getting out of debt, some folks find it overwhelming. Because they are looking at the destination it can seem too far off, but we want to look at debt demolition as little road signs along the way.

The destination is "getting out of debt" and the road signs will represent goals we must attain along the way to reach the destination.

If you are planning a trip, you first determine your destination. Then you decide which route or roads you will travel to get there as well as how long it will take to reach your destination.

Getting out of debt is the same way. You see your destination and now you plan the route and determine how long the trip will take. How long will it take to get there? This helps prepare you mentally and emotionally to endure the trip and maintain the energy to reach the goal.

If you are married, this is the time to have a meeting with your spouse. Discuss your desire and the importance of getting out of debt, so that you'll be able to take the necessary steps to build wealth.

> *"Can two walk together, unless they are agreed."*
>
> AMOS 3:3 NKJV

There is power in agreement!

> *"How could one chase a thousand, or two put ten thousand to flight."*
>
> DEUT 32:30 NKJV

There is exponential multiplication in agreement.

> *"Again I say to you that if two of you agree on earth concerning anything that they ask, it will be done for them by My Father in heaven."*
>
> MATT 18:19 NKJV

Agreement is powerful and results in **multiplication, not merely addition!**

If our prayers in agreement resulted in addition, then one would put a thousand to flight and two would put two thousand to flight. But we see in this Scripture, that praying in agreement results in multiplication.

God will get right in the middle of your goals when you are working on getting out of debt. He will be right there in the middle of your agreement.

> *"Again I say to you that if two of you agree on earth concerning anything that they ask, it will be done for them by My Father in heaven."*
>
> MATT 18:19 NKJV

The word "agree" is a Greek word "sumphoneo" and means "to agree in sound or to be in harmony." This is where we get the word symphony.

Two separate instruments, which make a completely different sound, come together and the sound together is more beautiful than the sound of one alone.

This is what prayer in unity and agreement looks like. Two separate people come together for a specific purpose. Each one contributes, yet blends with each other for a harmonic plan.

We have to be intentional and make a plan. If you want to demolish debt, then you must come up with a plan and set goals.

Here is a plan that you can follow.

8 Keys to Getting out of Debt

1. **Make a decision to stop borrowing money.**

    This may sound obvious, but if you want to get out of debt fast, you have to stop using debt to pay for your lifestyle. I've had some people say that they want to get out of debt, but intend to continue to utilize their credit cards. This is not the best way to get out of debt. True determination will result in the ceasing of using debt. You can't sign up for more credit cards, or finance another car, or charge new furniture. You have to stop acquiring new debts. This will enable you to focus on the debt you presently have and develop a plan to pay it off quickly.

Some folks have had the idea to reduce their payments each month by utilizing a consolidation loan. A consolidation loan is a debt that allows the consumer to pay off other debts. It combines credit card debts, personal loans, or other debts into one single bill that's paid off with one loan. The problem with this is if you haven't changed your habits of spending, you will not only have a consolidation loan, but will soon end up with other debts as well. The best way is to pay off each of your debts individually.

2. **Starter Emergency fund of $2000.**

    You might be thinking, "How am I supposed to get out of debt if I have to save $2000?" or "If I'm supposed to get out of debt, then shouldn't I just put that $2000 on my debt?" If you don't have any money in the bank and an emergency happens, then how will you pay for it? You don't want to use debt or credit cards to take care of your emergency.

    An emergency fund is just that—for emergencies. If something needs repaired or replaced, you will have the money to do so. If you find that you're in the middle of winter and your furnace needs replaced, you don't want to have to charge it. This will cause an emergency to become a crisis! An emergency fund allows you to take care of an emergency without having to go into debt to solve the issue. Eventually, you will want to have 6 months of living expenses in an emergency fund. Right now, the goal is $2000 in that fund until some debt is paid off.

3. **Create a budget.**

   A budget is telling your money what you want it to do. If you don't presently budget, then you may be a person that wonders where the money went at the end of the month.

   This will help you track your income and your expenses so you can get out of debt in a shorter period of time. It puts you in control of your money.

   A budget will reveal if you have money left over or if you have a negative at the end of the month.

   If you have money left over after all your bills, expenses are paid, then make sure you apply that "extra" money to the emergency fund until it's funded with $2000. If you already have the emergency fund in place, then apply that extra cash to your debts.

   If you are in the negative, then you're going to need to cut some of your expenses where you can and potentially work an extra job until you can afford to work just one job. There may be some items in your home or garage that you can sell to also apply that money to your debts. Remember, the goal is to get out of debt as quickly as possible.

   I've had some folks tell me they didn't want to work a second job or sell anything. I've coached people that swear they don't have anything to sell, yet their garage has four lawn mowers, and items in the basement or attic that are just collecting dust that they no longer use. How badly do you want out of the debt trap? Are you willing to sell some items? Are you willing to sell the boat that you only use on the weekends? Are you willing to do what you need to do?

4. **Organize your debts.**

   This key is an absolute must to paying off your debt. List all of your debts from smallest to highest. This is the "wrecking ball" approach. Pay off the smallest debt first, and then apply that payment to the next debt in line. This will build momentum. Just like a wrecking ball hits a building, it may take a few blows, but that building is coming down!

   Create a poster board for your office that lists all your debts and each time a payment is made, color in that particular debt with how much closer you are to paying it off. This is a powerful visual.

   God gave Abram a powerful visual. He changed his name from Abram to Abraham. The name Abraham means "father of a multitude." Abram didn't have any children yet, but God renamed him for a powerful illustration. He didn't have any children but God wanted Abraham to see himself the way God sees him. God wanted Abram to see himself as a father of a multitude. Every time Abraham saw the innumerable sands of the seashore, he was reminded of what God promised him! Every time Abraham saw the boundless stars in the sky he was reminded of what God had promised!

   What is God promising you in the area of finances? Where can you come into agreement with what God says about you? What vision can you place before your eyes? God sees you debt-free and prosperous! The Bible teaches us to write the vision that they may run that read it. Keeping the goal of debt freedom before your eyes, will enable you to move towards it!

Here are a few steps to help with this organizing process:

- When you begin, start with the budget. Look at your total take home pay for the month and write that down.
- Then write down every monthly bill you have. This will include housing, utilities, groceries, car payments, credit card payments, student loans, and any other debts you may have.
- Total the amount of payments toward each debt.
- Hopefully the debt payments for the month will be less than your take home pay. If it isn't, then you need to consider selling some items that you can get payment for or acquire a second job.
- This will help ensure that you make your payments each month.
- If you are able to make all of your payments and still have money leftover at the end of the month, then earmark that money for your emergency fund, until it is fully funded with $2000.
- Remember, money in an emergency fund will be available if an emergency arises.
- I recently coached someone about this very plan, and they didn't take the advice. A few weeks later their hot water tank had to be replaced.
- If they had the emergency fund, they would have had the money to pay for it and made this stressful situation no problem.
- But because he didn't have that money in place, he ended up using debt to buy the hot water tank, and created more debt and more stress!

- Once you have the emergency fund of $2000, then any extra money that is leftover at the end of the month, after paying all bills, needs applied to the lowest balance debt. This will ensure you get that paid off more quickly. Once that lowest balance debt is paid, then apply that payment to the next one in line.

- Keep applying those additional payments, so that you're demolishing those debts and working towards debt freedom.

- Remember that with each debt paid, it's a road sign getting you closer to debt freedom and wealth building.

5. **Practice couponing.**

   Don't shut me down on this one! Couponing can save you lots of money if done right. There are approximately over 300 billion coupons distributed each year, but only 2.2 billion were redeemed in 2016. I'm not saying to spend hours clipping coupons to save $1.99. But if you have a magazine or newspaper or access to online coupons, use them. Don't use coupons for things that you don't usually buy, unless you can get it for free. If it's not something you'll use, it's wasted money. Use coupons to your advantage.

6. **Put extra cash toward debts.**

   Once the credit card (or revolving line of credit) is paid off, you need to close the account and cut up the card! Then contact the card company and ask them to send you a letter stating the account is closed. You will want to place these letters in a folder in the event you would need to show proof of the closed account.

   The more cash you can put towards your debt, the faster it will disappear.

This also builds momentum. With each debt cancelled, have a celebration. Pop some popcorn and watch a movie, or go out to dinner, do something to celebrate each win you attain!

7. **Work towards having six months of living expenses in your emergency fund.**

    The goal is to pay off all debt, with the exception of your home, before you begin building up your emergency fund to hold six months of living expenses. Once the credit cards, personal loans, and student loans are paid off, then the goal will be to fill your emergency fund with enough money for you to live on for six months. Then if an emergency arises you are prepared. Some folks ask the reason for waiting to build up the six months living expenses. Your debts have much more interest on them than what you will get from a savings account. My husband and I both work and a year ago, he was laid off from his employment, which we thought would be a few weeks. He ended up being laid off for six months. We were thankful that we had more than enough in an emergency fund to cover. Preparation is key, so when something unexpected occurs, it doesn't turn into a crisis. Planning and budgeting is key to preparation!

8. **Pay yourself.**

    Once debts are paid (except the house) and you have a fully funded emergency fund, you can begin making more money go towards getting your mortgage paid off. Think how quickly this can happen. Now, you don't have credit cards, personal loans, student loans, or car payments. Now is the time to put that money with your house payment and watch the mortgage be annihilated. Imagine how far your money would go without a mortgage payment!

CHAPTER 6

Don't Be Passive About Your Income!

We must review what types of income are available. There is **earned income**, **portfolio income**, and **passive income**.

- **Earned income** is where you work for someone and they pay you wages for the job you do because you earned it. In this case, earned income is taxed around 50%.

- **Portfolio income** is from paper assets and capital gains. This income is taxed at 20%. Examples would be purchasing a house because it may increase in value, or purchasing stocks.

- **Passive income** is income that comes in on a regular basis and is taxed much lower, usually at 10% or less.

Simply put, passive income is income you earn without actively being involved. This means you continue to make income with no or little effort on your part to maintain that flow of cash.

Passive income will include regular earnings from somewhere other than an employer or contractor. At the time of this writing, the IRS says that **passive income can come from: rental income or a business in which a person doesn't have to actively participate. This will include book royalties and stocks that pay dividends.** Some investors will claim that flipping houses or wholesaling homes is passive income; however that is not the case. Remember that passive income is where you're not necessarily actively participating. We can discuss purchasing properties and then selling them for profit. This topic could be a book in itself, but let me give you some tips on what I have done in purchasing and selling properties.

Buying & Selling Properties

Many states have a State Auditor Office. State auditors are executive officers who serve as controllers and auditors of state funds. In West Virginia, they also handle properties that have been sold to the state for non-payment of property taxes. Within the state auditor office, there is a county collection division and their role is to return tax-delinquent lands to private ownership. This is accomplished through redemption of property and offering the parcels at public auction. You will want to check the status of properties in your own state.

In WV, once taxes on various properties have not been paid, the state auditor office will acquire the property as a tax lien and give the owners 18 months to redeem the property. If the property hasn't been redeemed, then after 18 months, they certify the property to the Deputy Land Commissioner for public auction. This is where you have the opportunity to purchase properties at a drastically reduced rate. Call your state auditor office for dates of the upcoming auctions and ensure you get to the auction early. They may be required to post the property addresses in the newspaper as well as on their website, so you'll have time before the auction to search them out.

In WV, properties will begin with the bidding of $10. Now, this isn't to say that the bid will stop there, but I have purchased properties for $10. The bidding may go up, depending on the location, if there is a building on the property etc.

Once all the bidding is complete, you pay for them in the tax office. In WV, the state auditor office will then send a letter of notification within 30 days to the buyers at the auction stating they approved the sale and also send some necessary paperwork. This paperwork will need filled out by an attorney. The attorney will do his due diligence and check if there are any heirs of the property. In WV, any relatives would need notified of the property being sold at auction and give them the opportunity to redeem the property. Most of the time, the properties remain unredeemed.

Then the attorney will send the state auditor office the paperwork and we wait. If the property is redeemed, the money spent at auction is refunded to you the buyer. If the property isn't redeemed, the auditor office will then send you a fee to be paid for recording of the deed. This may seem like a long process, but once you do this, it can be very lucrative. Once you have the deed in hand, the property is yours.

I once bought a property sight unseen (I don't recommend this) but I knew the general area. I paid $10 for the property, paid $300 to the attorney and paid $50 for the recorded deed. I ended up selling the property for $1400.

I also bought a house at auction for $700, paid $300 for the attorney, and $50 for the deed recording, and sold it for $5000. The house was in disarray, but was worth getting the $5000 for it.

Now, some of the properties may sell for much more. There was a large piece of property with several acres and in a prime location next to a shopping mall. The property was assessed and valued at $650,000 but the man who won the bid only paid $25,000 for it.

Purchasing properties at a state auditor auction is lucrative but requires patience. In WV, they hold this auction once a year in each county. So, you can actually do your research and perhaps go to various county auctions. I do recommend that you get the list of properties before the auction, as they will have a list, and take a day or two to see where the properties are located and what kind of condition they are in.

Rental Income

Let's talk about rental income. This isn't for the faint of heart. You must do your due diligence. Why would you want to invest in rental properties?

*TAX BENEFITS-

Investing in real estate allows for many tax benefits.

1. **Interest**—You can deduct interest from mortgage payments on loans. Certainly, I recommend that you pay cash for the property.

2. **Depreciation**—The owner can deduct the cost of the property over several years. It benefits your taxes by way of depreciation if the property is giving you an income.

3. **Repairs**—Any repairs are deductible in the year in which they are done. This enables you to deduct the cost of those repairs.

4. **Insurance**—You're able to deduct insurance premiums that have to do with your rental property. This includes liability, flood insurance, fire and theft.

*APPRECIATION-

Rental properties usually increase with inflation. So if inflation occurs, your rental income can increase. Real estate appreciation occurs when home values rise because of businesses, popularity of the area, or neighborhood growth. Think about homeowners that bought their home 20 years ago. They bought it for a good price, and now their home may be valued with $150,000 equity. Now, looking at rental property. Let's say you purchase a rental and rent it out for 20 years. This would be a great source of income and most likely has also increased in value.

*RETIREMENT INCOME-

Rental properties can be a great preparation for retirement income. Income from rental properties is considered passive income, but it doesn't mean that it's effortless. Purchasing rental property will not only create a great income for retirement, but also allows you to sell it at a higher price in the event you want to sell one of your rental properties.

So, how do you select a great rental property?

1. **Pick a great location.**

    Look for public transportation, schools, or proximity to major roads. What do the rentals in that area look like? Check the crime in that particular neighborhood. Most people don't want to live in a area of crime, and as the owner/landlord, you will want to avoid that. How much rent is being charged for them? If you're in a college, think like a student thinks. They want to be within walking distance of the college.

2. **Number of listings and vacancies.**

   If there's an unusually high listing in an area this can indicate either a seasonal cycle or a neighborhood that has gone bad. Vacancy rates can give you an idea of how successful you'll be attracting new tenants.

3. **Start small.**

   You are just beginning, and it's imperative that you do some research on rentals, the market in the area you plan on buying and checking your own financial situation to ensure you can afford it. Avoid properties needing significant repairs. In other words, don't bite off more than you can chew. Choose a property in a good location that doesn't need a lot of renovation. New carpet, some paint and a touch up out side for curb appeal is great.

   When you select a property that is run down, it may need new plumbing, electric, you get the picture.

4. **Run the numbers over and over again.**

   Don't assume that appreciation alone will be to your benefit. Rentals should have a positive cash flow and a good return. Don't forget to allot for property taxes and insurance. Check on the property taxes in your area. Most cities will double property taxes on rental properties as opposed to a home that's being acquired as the owner's residence.

5. **Choose tenants wisely!**

   As the buyer, are you going to be the property manager? Are you the one that is going to hand pick the tenant? Be prepared to have them fill out a rental application, do a credit check and a thorough interview with the potential tenant. Most investors say that a tenant should make at least three times the amount of rent. So if your rental can support $1000/month rent, then the income from the prospective tenant should be at least $3000 a month take home pay.

6. **Check the job market in the area.**

   Areas with growing employment opportunities may attract more people. If you know about a new major company moving to the area, then most likely there will be new folks moving to the area.

7. **Certificate of occupancy.**

   Check with the city in which you will be purchasing the property. Some cities will require a certificate of occupancy. There is a fee for this certificate as well as an inspection. Cities do this to ensure that the rental has appropriate smoke detectors, handrails, safe electric and a good habitation for the people that will reside there.

8. **Get a business license for rentals.**

   Before you purchase properties for rental income, contact your Secretary of State office, business division and acquire a business license for rentals. You will want to keep your rental income in a business for accounting and tax purposes.

9. **Have a lease agreement with your tenants.**

   Tenants should be required to not only fill out an application but provide you with references, personal, work and rental. They should provide you with a copy of their driver's license. A lease is imperative when renting to prospective tenants. I have a 6 page lease that covers details of the agreement between tenant and landlord. This not only protects the tenant but you as the owner. Although it's not mandatory, encourage the tenant to obtain insurance on their contents. Your rental insurance will NOT cover their contents. If a fire or flood were to occur, the insurance protects you as the owner for the property. It would benefit the tenant to get rental insurance on their personal property.

10. Foreclosures.

Some have asked about purchasing properties through foreclosure. You may check the newspaper ads for listings under foreclosure notices or auction sales. Check with lending institutions and government agencies; such as the Federal Housing Administration, or Department of Housing and Urban Development about foreclosed properties in your area.

> Once you have purchased the property, earning income can begin!

CHAPTER 7

Kids and Money

This particular chapter is going to cover money and children. Now some of you may be thinking, "Why in the world would this chapter be in a book that talks about motivation, methods, and manners regarding money?"

Children are going to learn about money from you. If you have kids, your actions and manners regarding money need to come from you!

The Word of God says:

> "Train up a child in the way he should go, and when he is old he will not depart from it."
>
> PROV 22:6 NKJV

Most people think this verse is talking about kids that are raised in the church and if they stray away then they will come back.

I'm not saying that this verse doesn't apply to that situation, but we need to look at the next verse to have an accurate understanding of what the writer is saying.

> "The rich rules over the poor, and the borrower *is* servant to the lender."
>
> PROV 22:7 NKJV, EMPHASIS ADDED

These two verses are saying that if we will train our children not to go into debt, then when they get older that will stay out of debt.

These verses are talking about money and how we are to train our children in regards to money!

We live in a culture where there is such a sense of entitlement among so many kids, young adults, and even older adults.

They have marches, pickets, and are very passionate about someone else paying for things—like their college should be free, their healthcare should be free, etc. Can I tell you that these things are NOT FREE?!

Many have the mindset that the government should pay for these things. It's not the government's job to pay for your children's education, because it's not free. Working people like you and me end up paying taxes to the government.

The government doesn't have money unless they tax folks.

Okay, rant over.

What I am trying to say is that kids are going to learn about money from you and the earlier you start the better.

Some parents pay their children an allowance and don't attach any expectation to that payment.

Are we paying our kids money for just existing?

Let's not pay an allowance, but rather a commission.

That word even sounds better, doesn't it?

We need to attach work with money, because God expects us to work. In fact, that is one of the first things He did with Adam and Eve. He gave them a job to tend the garden, take care of it. See work is good!

God called the garden and everything He created good. Then He gave Adam and Eve work to do. If you will begin by teaching your children work is good and when we work we get paid, it will reset their thinking in regards to money.

I am one of seven children, so we had a house filled with nine people ... talk about living an interesting life, we had only one bathroom! To this day, I still can't recall how that worked out. But one of the great things my parents did was that they assigned each one of us chores to do.

Now, there were certain chores we did that we did not get paid. Why? Because we lived in their house and therefore needed to contribute to the household. That should be the case in your own home as well.

Because they are a part of the Smith family, or your family, there should be chores or tasks that are normal that don't require payment from you. This could be making their bed daily, keeping their room cleaned, vacuuming. Whatever those tasks are, set them up and require those things to be done by them.

When they start a job in the workforce, they will have the mindset to do things over and beyond what is required and this will cause them to get ahead and their boss to take notice of them.

There may be certain chores around your home that you decide are worthy or payment or commission. You get to decide.

It may be if they mow the lawn, they get $10 or if they clean out the garage and organize it, they may get $20, or if they do laundry, set an amount accordingly. Now this is all depends on how large your lawn is, or how long it will take to organize that garage.

Make a list of the tasks or chores that you want done and place the payment amount next to it. Let your children know that you will no longer be paying them an allowance (entitlement), but they will be able to earn money, through commissions, and explain the chart you have created with the tasks and payments.

"If anyone will not work, neither shall he eat."

2 THESS 3:10B NKJV

The Word of God tells us that we should work! Following this principle in your own home will not only alleviate you from doing everything, but it will give them a sense of self-worth, because now they are working to get paid.

Why Kids Should Work

- It keeps them busy and challenges them to develop themselves.
- It gives them a sense of pride and achievement.
- It causes them to socialize and causes them to learn to work well with others.
- It provides them with money that will allow them to make their own purchases, which also gives them a sense of self-worth.

This is such a brief list of why children should work, but you can see the benefits.

Now I have been asked how young should you start?

Children as young as four years old can grasp this concept. Encourage them and allow them to make some mistakes along the way.

Will they make their bed perfect? No, but we all have to start somewhere.

I can recall when I was six years old, my mother lowering the ironing board to my height and she taught me how to iron my dad's handkerchiefs. They were square and she set the iron on the correct setting and showed me how.

This gave me a sense of pleasure because I was permitted to do something I had never done and when I finished ironing them I had a great sense of accomplishment.

Kids need to be challenged and I was certainly challenged that day, but oh what a work ethic I have today.

You will instill such a great work ethic in them, that they will want to work, and anything contrary to work, they will repel.

Will they like it when you explain that they will no longer be getting an allowance but have an opportunity to get paid?

No, most likely they won't embrace this new concept, but you will be doing your job as a parent that is instilling in them the necessities of work and attaching commissions with work.

A powerful visual is to make 3 separate clear containers appropriately marked as follows:

- **GIVING**
- **SAVING**
- **SPENDING**

Since they will be earning a commission rather than an allowance, there should be a set "payday" for them. You like getting paid the same day each week, so will your children.

Make the three separate containers with the labels and teach them to give some, save some, and they can even have a jar for spending.

This will instill in them the importance of returning to the Lord the tithe. (This is mentioned earlier in this book.) It will also teach and train them to begin saving and not to spend every dollar they make.

Of course, they will have the wonderful benefit of spending some of their hard earned money and re-emphasize the gratification they will get by working and earning money.

> If we train our children to work, earn, and not go into debt, when they are adults they will know how to work, earn, and not go into debt

Final Word

It is my hope that by reading through this book, you have not only answered the question if God wants you to have money (He does!), but also comprehend that He has a desire for you to build wealth.

This book gives multiple keys to debt demolition as well as principles to building wealth.

Truly, money does matter!

You may have read this book for a variety of reasons, and may not know God or have a personal relationship with Him. If you don't know Him and would like to begin this relationship, then I invite you to pray this prayer right now.

> God, I don't know you but I want to. I understand that I am a sinner and I ask that you forgive me of my sins and make me new. I ask that you come into my heart, and as you do, I begin a new life in Christ. Thank you Lord for forgiving me and cleansing me. In Jesus, name I pray, amen.

If you prayed this prayer for the first time, then let me hear from you. Send me a message through my website.

www.karenford.org

KBF MONEY MANAGING

Do you need help eliminating debt, planning cash flow, and building wealth? As a Master Certified Financial Coach, Karen Ford's money managing techniques will guide you into living debt free. She will help you create and execute budgeting strategies and tackle planning for retirement as you build wealth for your future. Karen offers seminars and coaching for the following:

- keys for debt demolition
- cash flow planning
- how to retire well
- how to build wealth

For information on coaching services, seminars, or to invite Karen to speak, please visit:

www.karenford.org

www.ingramcontent.com/pod-product-compliance
Lightning Source LLC
Chambersburg PA
CBHW070438010526
44118CB00014B/2101